FOR THE BIRDS!
A Book About Air

by  Jill Wheeler

Illustrated by Angela Kamstra
and
Krista Schaeppi

Published by Abdo & Daughters, 4940 Viking Drive,Suite 622, Edina, Minnesota 55435.

Library bound edition distributed by Rockbottom Books, Pentagon Towers, P.O. Box 36036, Minneapolis, Minnesota 55435.

Interior Photograph - Wide World

Edited by Julie Berg

LIBRARY OF CONGRESS CATALOGING-IN-PUBLICATION DATA
Wheeler, Jill C., 1964 -
    For the birds : a book about air / written by Jill Wheeler.
        p.   cm. -- (Target earth)
    Summary: Discusses air pollution and suggests things we can do to help clean our air.
    ISBN 1-56239-196-8
    1. Air -- Pollution -- Juvenile literature. 2. Air quality management -- Juvenile literature. 3. Air -- Juvenile literature. [1. Air -- Pollution. 2. Pollution.] I. Title. II. Series.
    TD883.13.W55 1993
    363.73'92--dc20
    [B]   93-7751
                               CIP
                               AC

Thanks To The Trees From Which This Recycled Paper Was First Made.

Table of Contents

Let's Begin Here.

Most people don't think often about air. We breathe air from the moment we're born. We inhale about 3,000 gallons (11,280 liters) of air a day. People can live weeks without food. They can live days without water. They can live only a few minutes without air.

Humans breathe air for the oxygen it contains. Our lungs transfer the oxygen to our blood. Our heart pumps that blood through our bodies. The oxygen-rich blood feeds our cells. We exhale, or breathe out, the unused part of the air.

Even fish need oxygen to live. They get oxygen from water. They have gills to take the oxygen out of the water.

Yet fish don't pollute. People are the only creatures who pollute the air. People also are the only ones who can stop pollution. If we want to save the Earth, we must begin now. If we don't take action, the air will only get worse. Our children and grandchildren will suffer.

This book will tell you about air pollution. It will tell what you can do to help clean the air. There are many simple actions you can take every day. Soon these actions will become a habit. If many people take these actions, the air will get better. It won't happen immediately. But it can happen. It took many years for the air to become polluted. It will take time for it to get clean again.

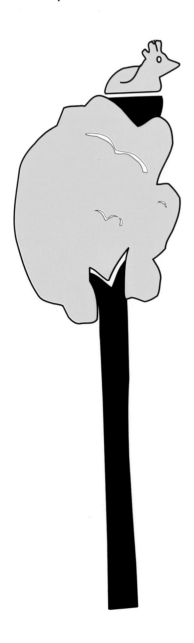

Did You Know...

One acre (.4 hectares) of trees can absorb lots of carbon dioxide. It can absorb as much as a car makes driving 26,000 miles (41,600 kilometers).

Something's in the Air

The Earth was very different millions of years ago. Most scientists believe there was no air then. They believe there were just different kinds of gases. These gases swirled together between the land and outer space. There was no *oxygen* for living creatures to breathe.

Little by little, air developed. It formed when sunlight mixed with the gases. The new air contained oxygen and *nitrogen*. The air kept forming for many years. Finally, there was enough air to support plants and animals.

Even then, the air was not all clean. Ancient volcanos often erupted. The volcanos shot streams of hot gases and molten rock into the air. Other times bolts of lightning started forest fires. These fires filled the air with smoke.

The first people on Earth also polluted the air. They used fire to heat the places where they lived. They used fire to cook food.

Yet no one minded the smoke from their fires. There were only a few people on Earth then. Winds quickly scattered what little smoke the people made.

As time went by, more people lived on the Earth. More people meant more pollution.

Did You Know...

Pollution is not a new problem. The Bay of Smokes near Los Angeles and Tierra del Fuego (Land of Fire), an island off the South American coast, both were named many years ago because of their polluted air.

Pollution Progression

Pollution has always been a part of life. For example, the Phoenicians lived more than two thousand years ago. They lived by the Mediterranean Sea. They made their living from the sea. They created a beautiful purple dye from shellfish. It smelled terrible when they made the dye. This was an early form of air pollution.

Years later, the Roman people lived in what is now Italy. The Romans wore brilliant white clothes called togas. They complained polluted air made their togas dirty. They may also have complained about how their city smelled. They did not have garbage collectors then. They also did not have sewer systems. They had to live with the smell of their own wastes. This included human waste, animal waste and food scraps.

A thousand years later, people in England became concerned about their air. They had cut down all the trees near their cities. They burned the trees for light and heat. They did not plant new trees to replace what they used. So they had to burn soft coal instead.

Smoke from coal fires is worse than smoke from wood fires. Coal-fire smoke stings the eyes and the throat. Many English people complained about how bad the coal smoke made them feel. So King Edward I of England passed a law in 1272. The law forbade people to burn soft coal. Sadly, few people obeyed the law. Years later, the law was stiffened. It said people could even be killed for burning coal. That still didn't stop people from burning the coal.

The problem grew worse during the 1700s. This was the time of the *Industrial Revolution*. The Industrial Revolution began in England. It spread across Europe and the United States. Factories began making many new products. These products made life easier for many people.

Making these products also created air pollution. Factories poured tons of poisonous gases and soot into the air. These gases made the air smell very bad. It caused people to cough. Some people had trouble breathing.

At the same time, there were more and more people. More people meant more homes to heat. It meant more garbage to burn. Air pollution grew.

Air pollution in Europe became so bad people died. Many other people became sick. They had diseases like emphysema and lung *cancer*. Others had been sick even before the air became bad. They had diseases like asthma, bronchitis and heart disease. The polluted air made them feel even worse.

When people began dying from bad air, scientists coined the word *smog*. Smog is a mixture of smoke and fog. Smog was becoming common in the British Isles. There, pollutants from heavy industry mixed with the foggy weather.

Then the 1900s arrived. People began driving gasoline-powered automobiles. These cars made it easy for people to travel. The *emissions* from the cars also polluted the air. More people died from bad air.

Finally, people became concerned. They decided something had to be done about air pollution. That fight continues to this day.

Air Today, Gone Tomorrow

Few people die from killer smogs today. Anti-pollution laws have helped. Laws make factories filter the air coming from their smokestacks. Cars have new devices to reduce pollutants. In the United States, unleaded fuel has nearly replaced leaded fuel. Unleaded fuel releases fewer pollutants when burned.

But the air pollution problem is not yet solved. People continue to pollute the air in many ways.

We pollute the air when we buy household chemicals. These include floor wax, window cleaner, furniture polish and air fresheners. These products are made from chemicals. When factories make the chemicals, they release air pollutants.

We pollute the air when we operate vehicles. These include cars, trucks, vans, buses, motorcycles, mopeds, motorboats and airplanes. Cars create more pollution than any other source.

Did You Know...

The average American car emits its own weight in carbon each year. Carbon is a pollutant. It is created by burning gasoline.

We pollute the air when we buy things made of metal, paper, plastic and chemicals. Factories that make these items create pollution. These factories are the world's second largest source of pollution.

We pollute the air when we heat and cool our homes, and fix dinner. We pollute the air when we listen to our stereos and play computer games. All of these activities require energy. This energy usually comes from electricity, natural gas or fuel oil. Creating this energy pollutes the air.

We cannot stop polluting completely. People in cold climates would freeze to death without heat. And everyone must eat. Yet there are ways to live and still create less pollution.

Pollution is hurting people, plants and animals. Just look at what pollution is doing to the environment now.

Air pollution means fewer sunny days. Air pollution means many ancient statues and monuments are being ruined. We can never replace them. Air pollution means more people get colds and other diseases. Air pollution also makes animals and plants sick.

Did You Know...

Acid rain happens when pollution mixes with clouds. It then falls back to the Earth as rain, snow or fog.

Dark, grimy smog has bothered people for many years. Yet there are other problems caused by air pollution, too. Scientists are just now learning about these problems. We can't even see many of these threats. They include acid rain, losing the ozone layer, global warming and *toxic* chemicals. All of them can hurt us and our future.

Acid rain happens when pollution mixes with clouds. It then falls back to Earth as rain, snow or fog. This pollution comes from motor vehicles. It also comes from coal-burning electric companies.

Acid rain harms fish and wildlife. It has poisoned more than 1,500 large lakes. Acid rain has harmed thousands of acres (thousands of hectares) of forests. Nearly 100,000 people die each year because of acid rain. Acid rain hurts many buildings, statues and grain fields, too.

Losing the *ozone* layer is another problem. Ozone is a pure form of oxygen. It forms an invisible shield high above the Earth.

The shield protects the Earth from dangerous rays from outer space. These rays can give people can skin cancer or cataracts. It can make their bodies unable to fight off diseases. The rays also kill the algae fish eat, so there are fewer fish.

In 1985, scientists discovered a giant hole in the ozone layer. The hole was above the continent of Antarctica. Scientists think the hole is as deep as the highest mountain. They think it's as big as the United States.

Scientists think *chlorofluorocarbons*, or CFCs, caused the ozone hole. CFCs are chemicals used in spray cans and refrigeration systems. Many CFCs have been banned in the U.S. Other countries, however, still use them.

Global warming is also called the *Greenhouse Effect*. It happens when heat-trapping gases enter the air. These gases absorb the sun's rays. They hold the sun's heat within the Earth's *atmosphere*. Normally, this heat escapes into space.

Most global warming comes from *carbon dioxide*. Cars, trucks, power plants, factories and homes all emit carbon dioxide. Carbon dioxide in the air has grown since the Industrial Revolution. It has increased 25 percent.

The Earth needs some warmth from the sun to live. Yet too much heat causes problems. It can cause crops to fail. It can make water levels increase and cause flooding. Big changes in the climate affect plant, animal and human life. Some scientists believe the Earth is warming-up already. The four hottest years of the past 100 happened in the 1980s.

Toxic chemicals are common today. Many pesticides, herbicides and fertilizers contain toxic chemicals. People use these chemicals to kill weeds and insects. Some are used to make crops grow better. Sadly, some of the chemicals hurt the workers who apply them.

Chemicals can kill others, too. This happened in Bhopal, India, in 1984. A gas leak at a pesticide plant killed more than 5,000 people. The gas injured hundreds of thousands more.

Lawmakers have banned some of these chemicals in the United States. Some U.S. companies still make and sell the chemicals to other countries. These countries use the chemicals to grow food. This food can end up in U.S. grocery stores and on our plates.

As a safety precaution, workmen spray water on a fence that surrounds the chemical factory in Bhopal, India, in hopes of trapping the gas.

17

We want A clean House Not A Greenhouse.

No one can stop polluting the air completely. Yet we can do a little each day. We can improve the quality of the air we breathe.

If you use less energy, power companies will create less air pollution. You can use less energy to heat, cool and light your house. You can use less energy to prepare your food and take care of your clothes, too. Using less energy will help the ozone. It will also help prevent acid rain and reduce global warming. Here's how to use less energy.

In the winter, close the blinds or curtains of your bedroom at night. Open them on sunny days.

In the summer, close the blinds or drapes on sunny days. Open the windows at night to cool the house down.

Turn the heat down to 65 degrees Fahrenheit (18 degrees Celsius) at night. Turn it down, too, when no one's home.

18

Did You Know...

Hanging your clothes on a clothesline saves you 100% of the energy used by a clothes dryer. Your clothes will smell better and last longer too!

Turn the air conditioning up to 78 degrees Fahrenheit (26 degrees Celsius) in the summer. Wear shorts and a T-shirt in the house to stay cool.

Always turn off the lights when you leave a room.

Plant a tree. Trees remove carbon dioxide from the air. They also add oxygen to the air.

Eat foods like sandwiches and salads. These don't require heating the oven.

Ask your family to use storm doors and windows. Tell them insulation will help save energy.

If you have a clothesline, hang your clothes out to dry. Don't use the dryer.

Urge your family not to use chemical household cleaners. Clean with a mixture of ammonia, water, vinegar and baking soda instead.

Did You Know...

2.6 billion pounds (1.2 billion kilograms) of pesticides are applied to American fruits and vegetables every year. So please wash your fruits and vegetables well before eating them.

You're an Eco-Vehicle

Cars and trucks are the worst offenders in the pollution game. Follow these guidelines to use cars and trucks less. When you must use them, use them more efficiently.

 Ride your bicycle. Walk whenever you can.

 Use public transportation.

 Share rides with friends.

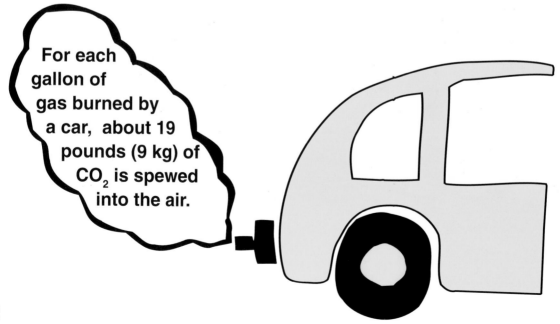

For each gallon of gas burned by a car, about 19 pounds (9 kg) of CO_2 is spewed into the air.

Did You Know...

If one out of 100 American car owners left their car at home once a week, it would save 42 million gallons (151 million liters) of gas a year.

🐦 Plan your day so you can do several things on one trip. Avoid many short trips.

🐦 Encourage others in your family to carpool. Or, urge them to use public transportation.

🐦 Check the air in the tires of your car. Full tires improve gas mileage.

🐦 Tell your family to purchase energy-efficient vehicles. Keep the engines tuned-up so they run like they should.

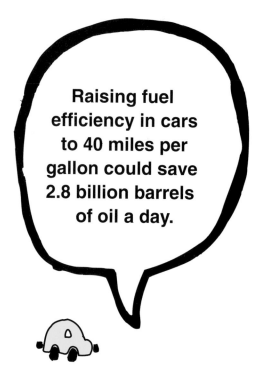

Raising fuel efficiency in cars to 40 miles per gallon could save 2.8 billion barrels of oil a day.

Save The Air at school

Get your classmates involved in the fight for clean air.

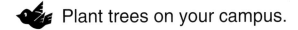 Plant trees on your campus.

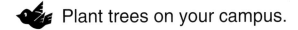 Get your school to offer classes on the environment. Have the teachers tell how to save the Earth.

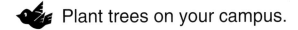 Organize a special travel day. Have teachers and students take the bus or carpool to school.

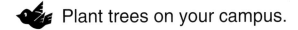 Keep up on environmental news with your classmates. Write letters to elected officials. Ask them to support legislation for better air.

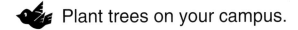 Ask your teacher and classmates to help with an Environmental Fair. Use exhibits to show the problems of air pollution. (For more information, see the Target Earth Earthmobile book *Eco-Fairs and Carnivals.*

Then show what everyone can do to help.

Did You Know...

Planting a tree helps clean the air.

And Remember:

If you could convince two of your friends to stop doing something that's harming the environment, then the next day, each of them convinced two friends and so on, the word would spread to everyone in the United States in less than one month.

Care about the Air

This book is filled with sad news about what people have done to our air. Since the beginning of time, we have found ways to pollute. But as this book shows, all is not lost. Scientists are learning more about the environment. They know what causes acid rain and global warming. They understand many other environmental problems. They know the causes of the problems. They can tell us how to stop these problems.

Along with the bad news, this book has good news. It shows ways you can improve the air you breathe. Remember the helpful hints in this book. Do what you can to help stop pollution. Ask people to follow your example. If enough people do, someday there may be no pollution problem at all.

Glossary

Acid Rain — Pollution mixing with clouds and falling back to the Earth in the form of rain.

Cataract — A disease of the eye.

Chlorofluorocarbons (CFCs) — A group of compounds that contain the elements carbon, chlorine, fluorine and sometimes hydrogen. They are used to make plastics and other solutions.

Cancer (Lung and Skin) — Diseases that can be caused by hazardous waste.

Carbon Dioxide — A colorless and odorless gas that is made up of carbon and oxygen.

Emissions — Substances discharged into the air (as by a smokestack or a car's engine).

Greenhouse Effect/Global Warming — The warming of the Earth's surface and the lower layers of the atmosphere.

Industrial Revolution — A rapid major change in a country's economy.

Nitrogen — A gas that has no color or smell. Nitrogen makes up almost four-fifths of the air on the Earth.

Organism — A living plant or animal.

Oxygen — A gas that has no color or smell. Oxygen makes up one-fifth of the air on the Earth.

Ozone Layer — The upper layer of the Earth's atmosphere containing ozone gas that blocks out the sun's harmful ultraviolet rays.

Pollution — Harming the environment by putting man-made wastes in the air, water and ground.

Respiratory Diseases — (Emphysema, Asthma, Bronchitis) Illnesses that affect the lungs.

Smog — A combination of smoke and fog in the air. Smog is found especially over cities or areas where there are factories.

Toxic — Harmful and poisonous.

Index

TARGET EARTH™ COMMITMENT

At Target, we're committed to the environment. We show this commitment not only through our own internal efforts but also through the programs we sponsor in the communities where we do business.

Our commitment to children and the environment began when we became the Founding International Sponsor for Kids for Saving Earth, a non-profit environmental organization for kids. We helped launch the program in 1989 and supported its growth to three-quarters of a million club members in just three years.

Our commitment to children's environmental education led to the development of an environmental curriculum called Target Earth™, aimed at getting kids involved in their education and in their world.

In addition, we worked with Abdo & Daughters Publishing to develop the Target Earth™ Earthmobile, an environmental science library on wheels that can be used in libraries, or rolled from classroom to classroom.

Target believes that the children are our future and the future of our planet. Through education, they will save the world!

TARGET®

Minneapolis-based Target Stores is an upscale discount department store chain of 517 stores in 33 states coast-to-coast, and is the largest division of Dayton Hudson Corporation, one of the nation's leading retailers.